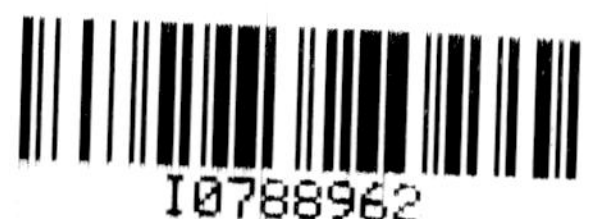

Coloring book for adults and kids
amazing lamb design

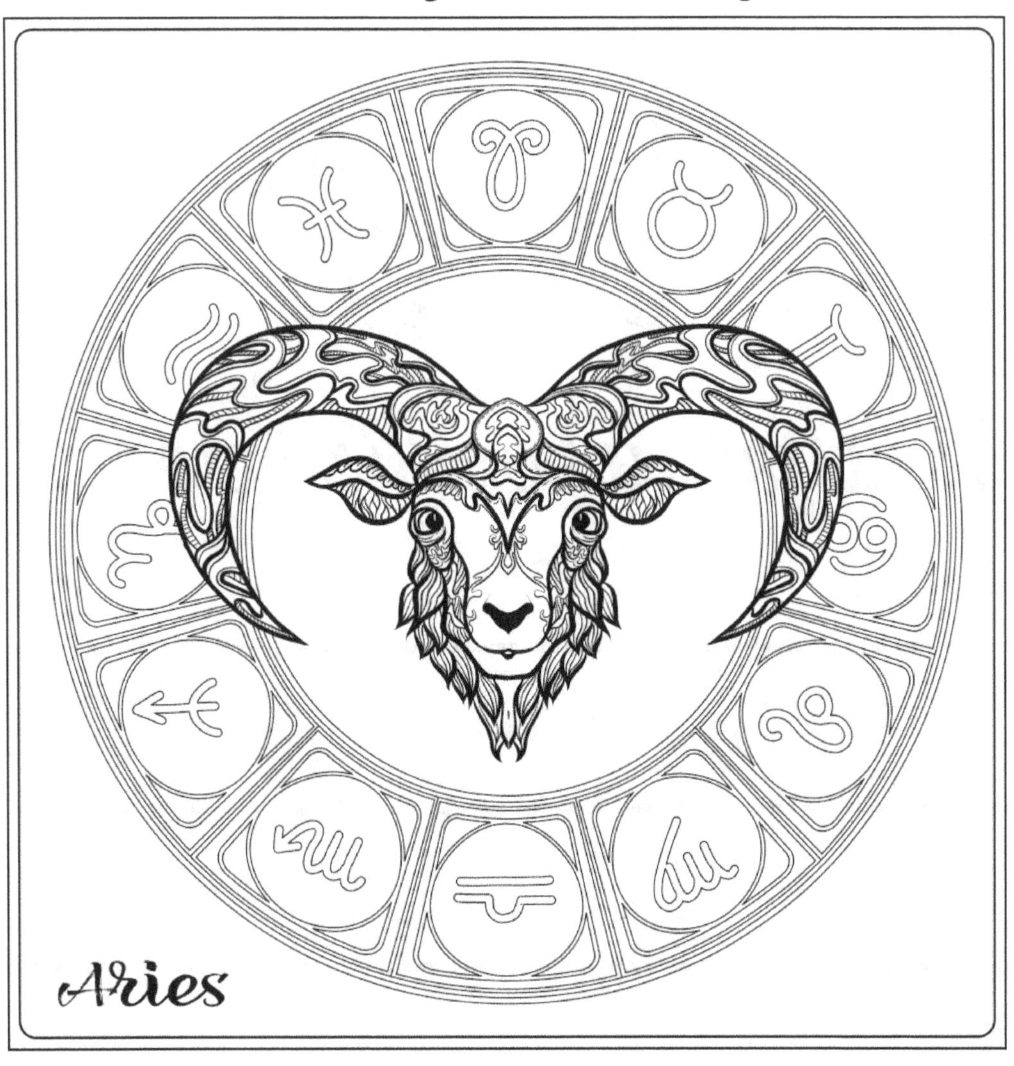

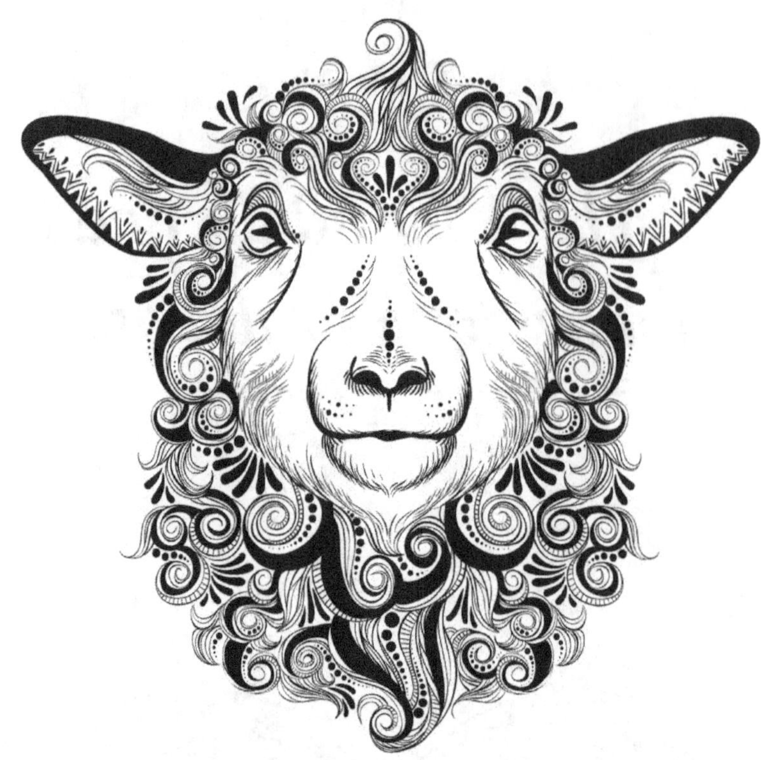

This coloring book is belongs to

____

____

____

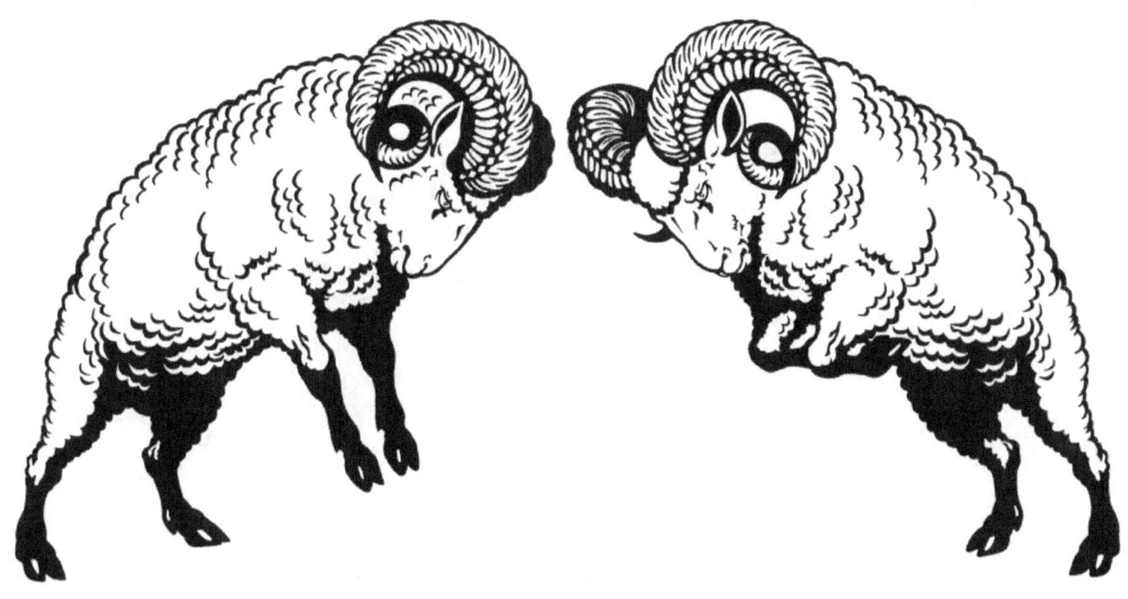

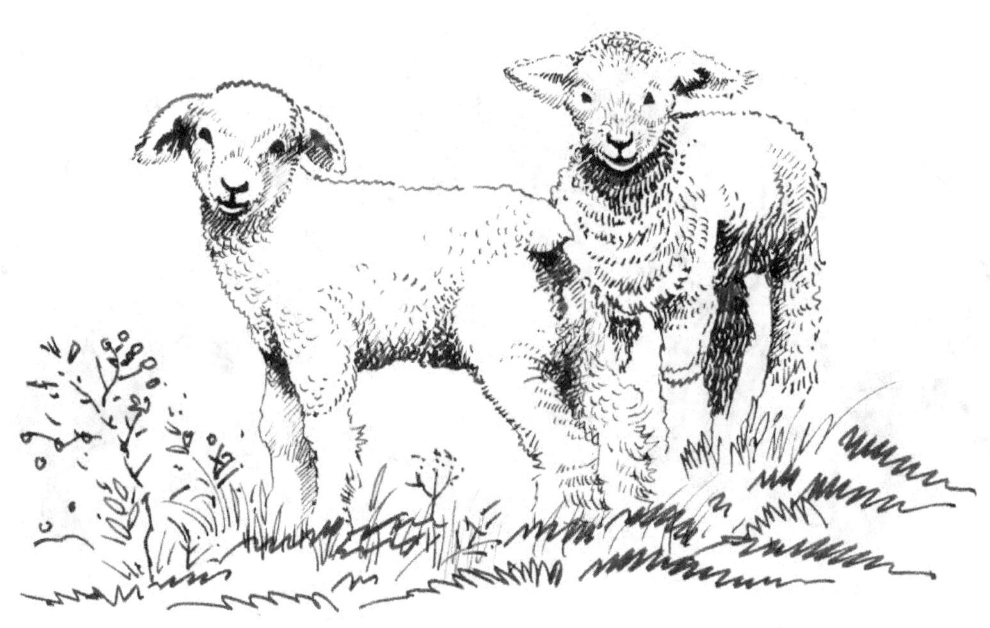

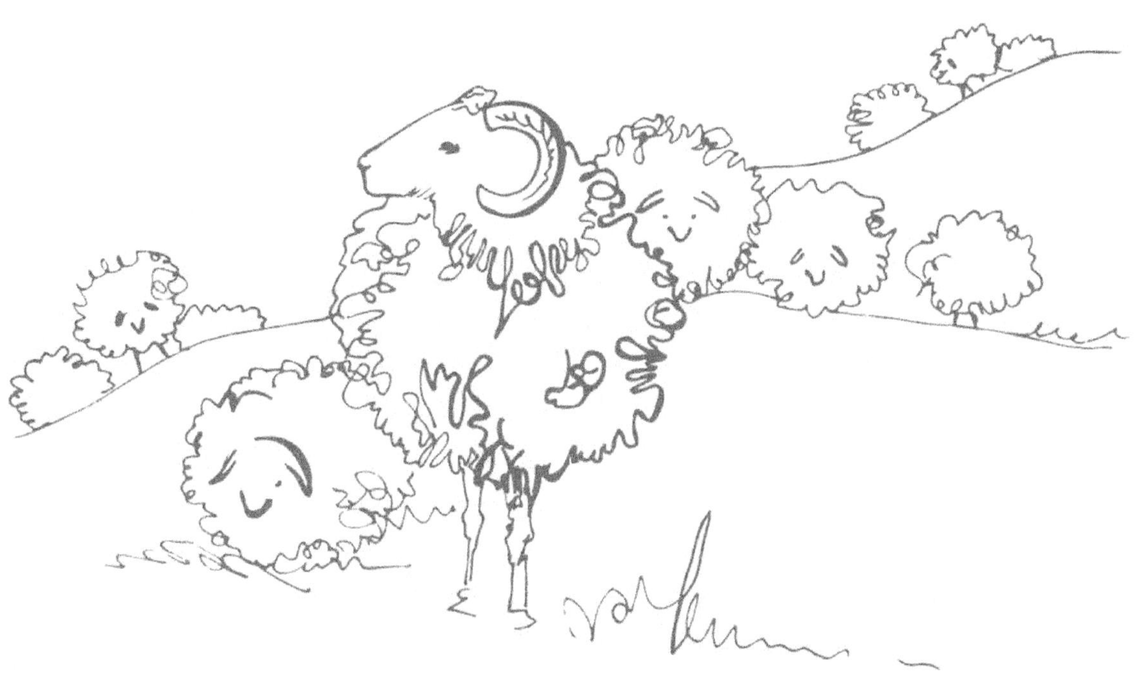

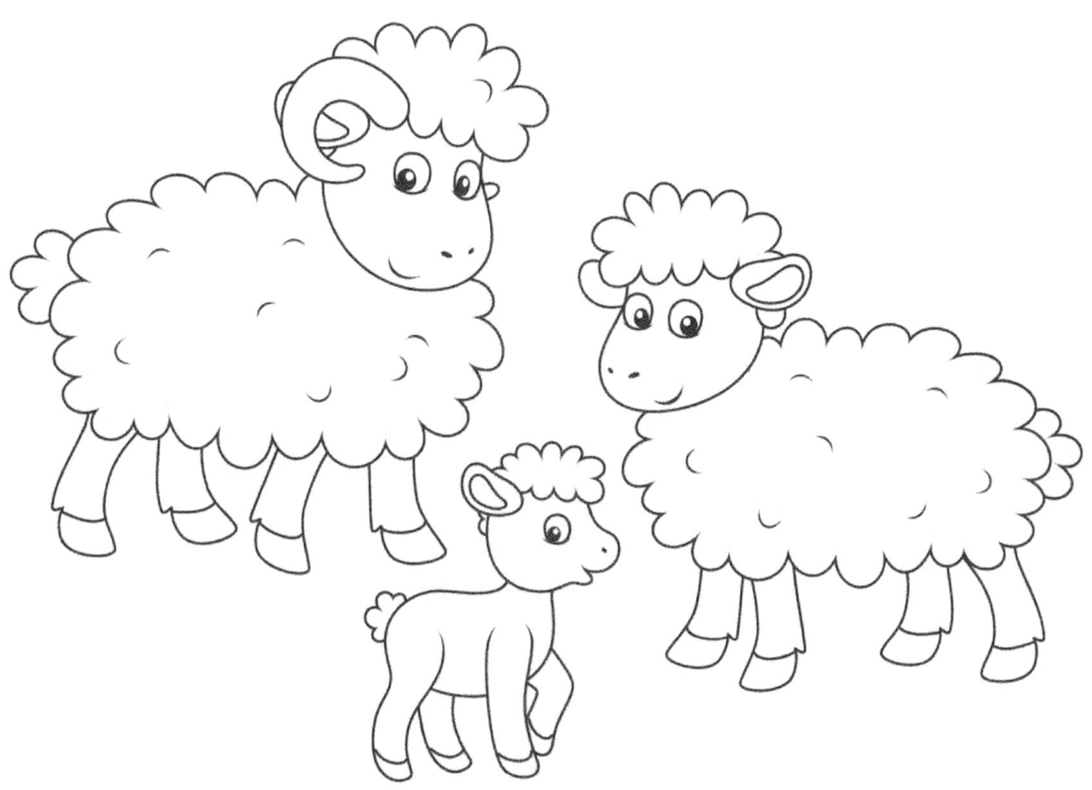

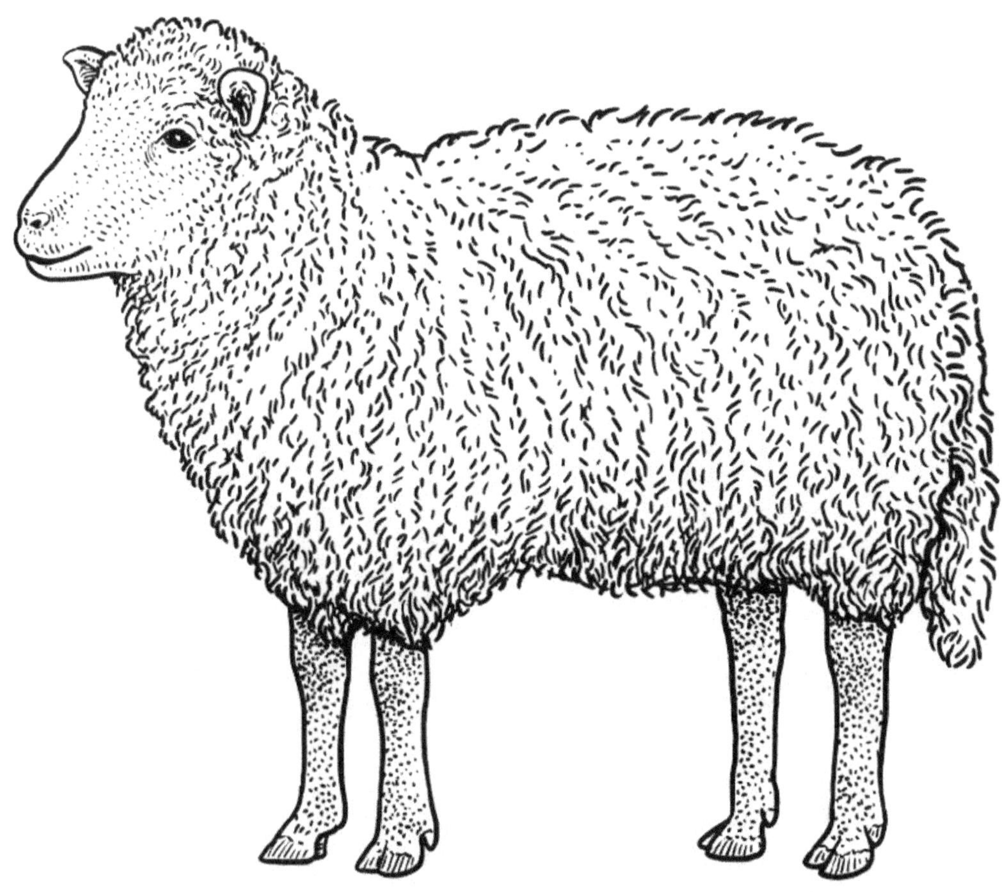

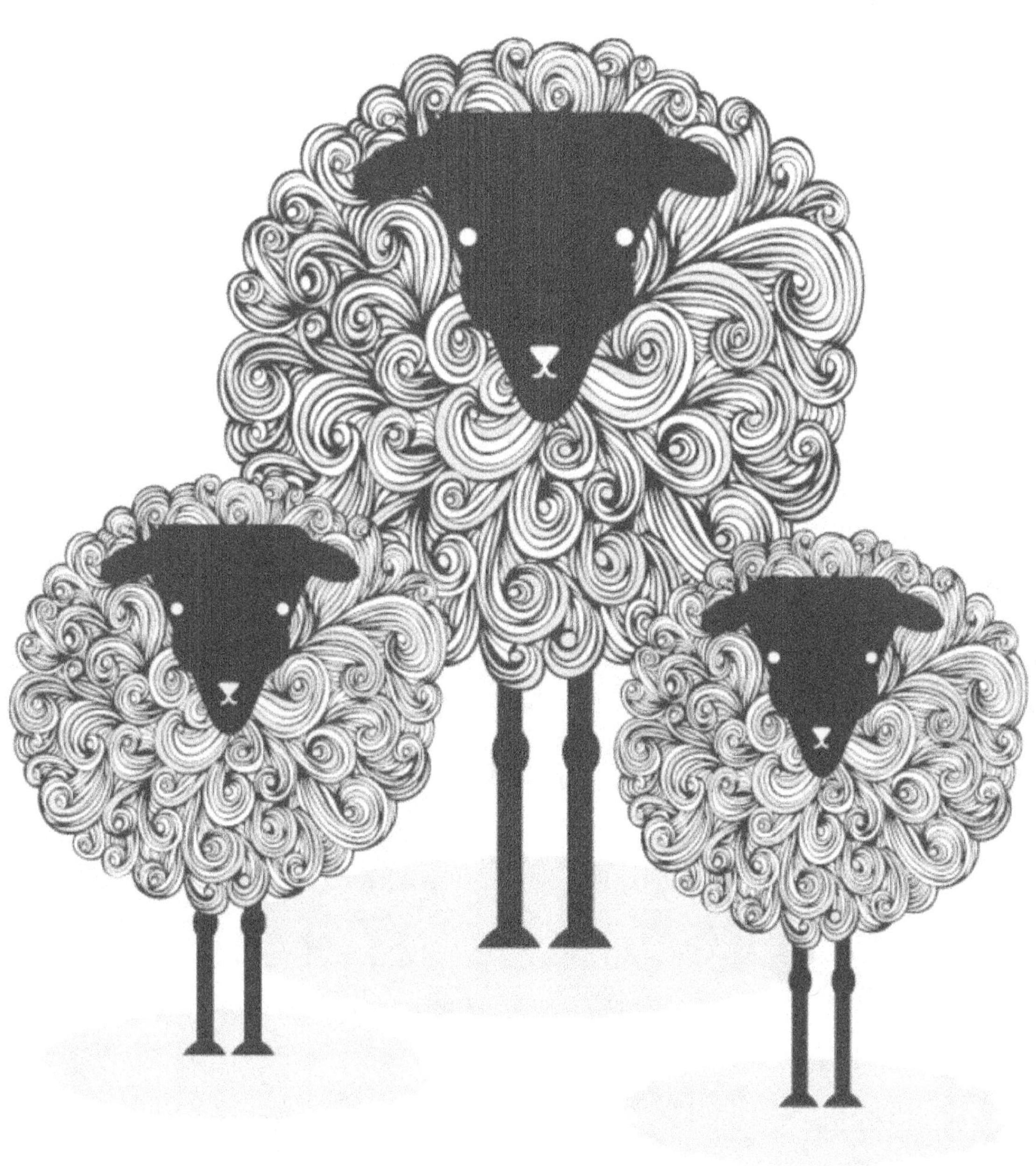

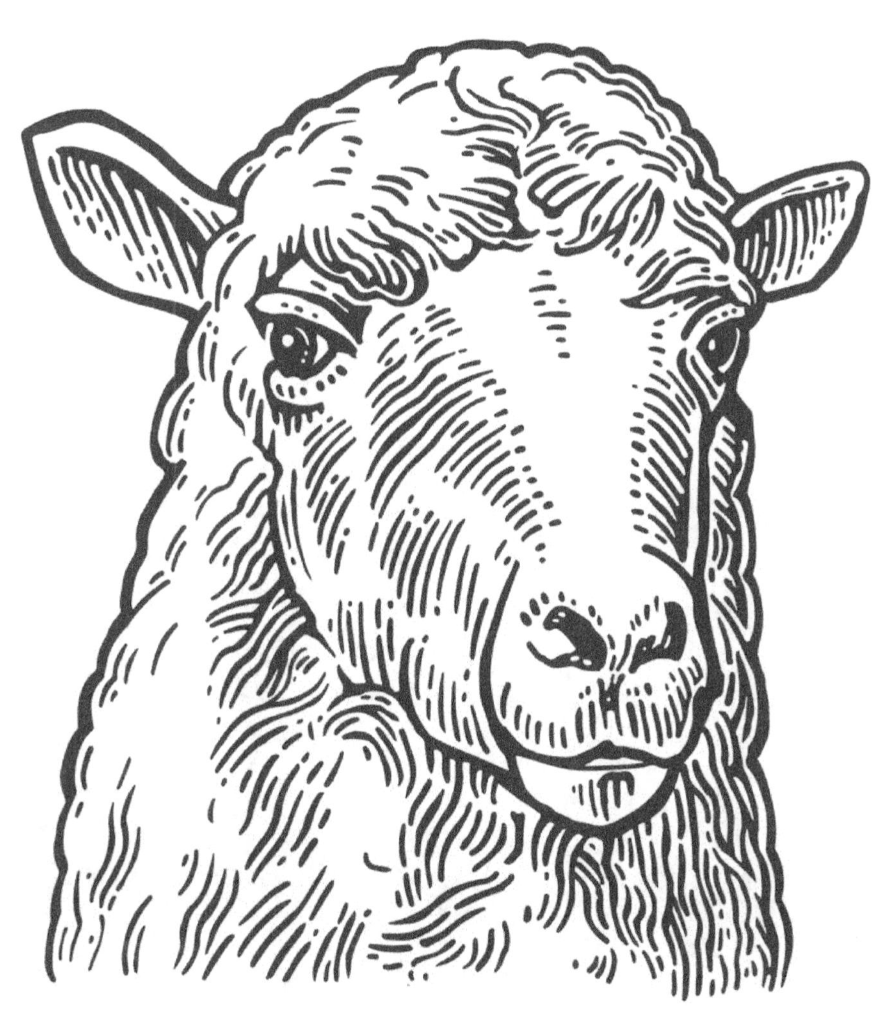

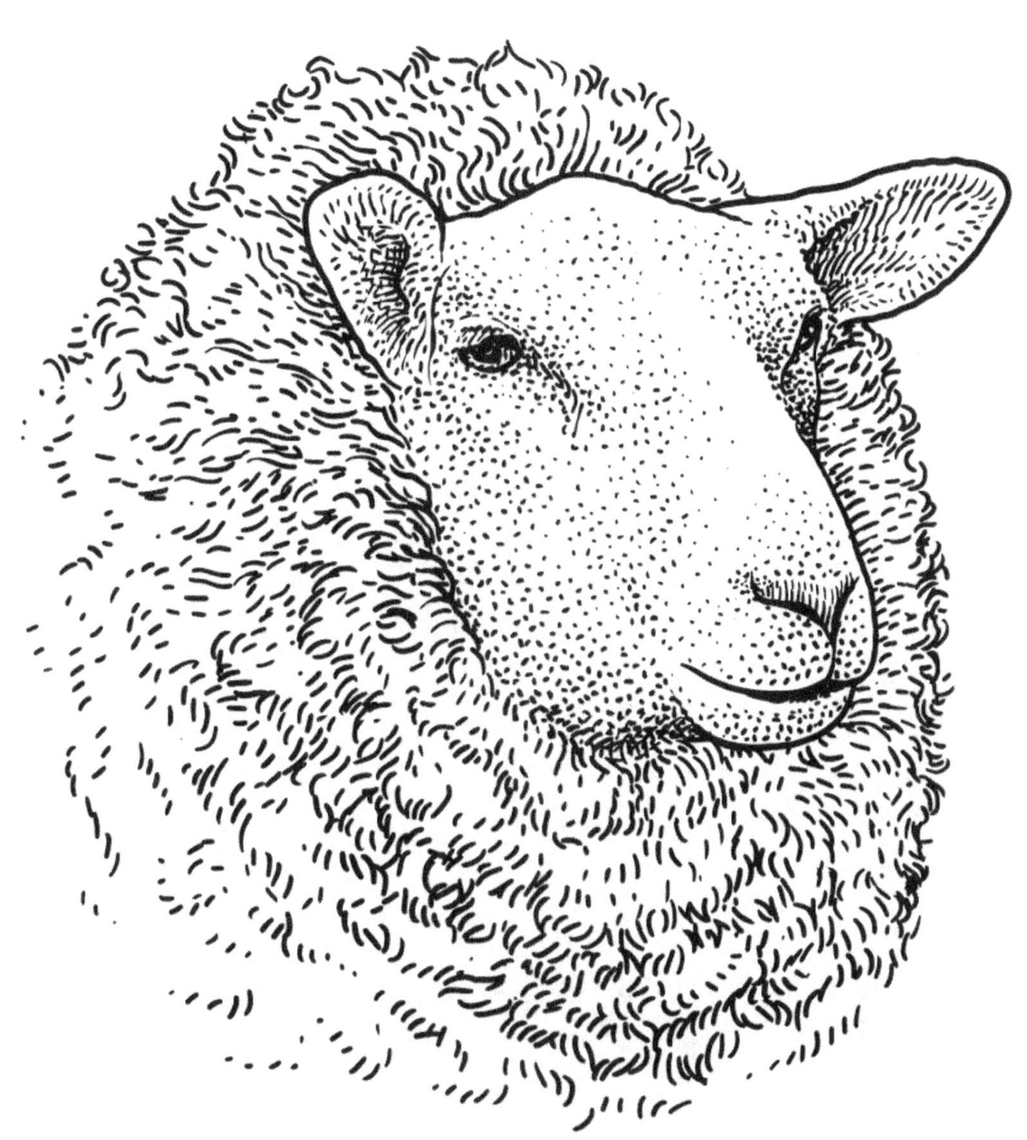

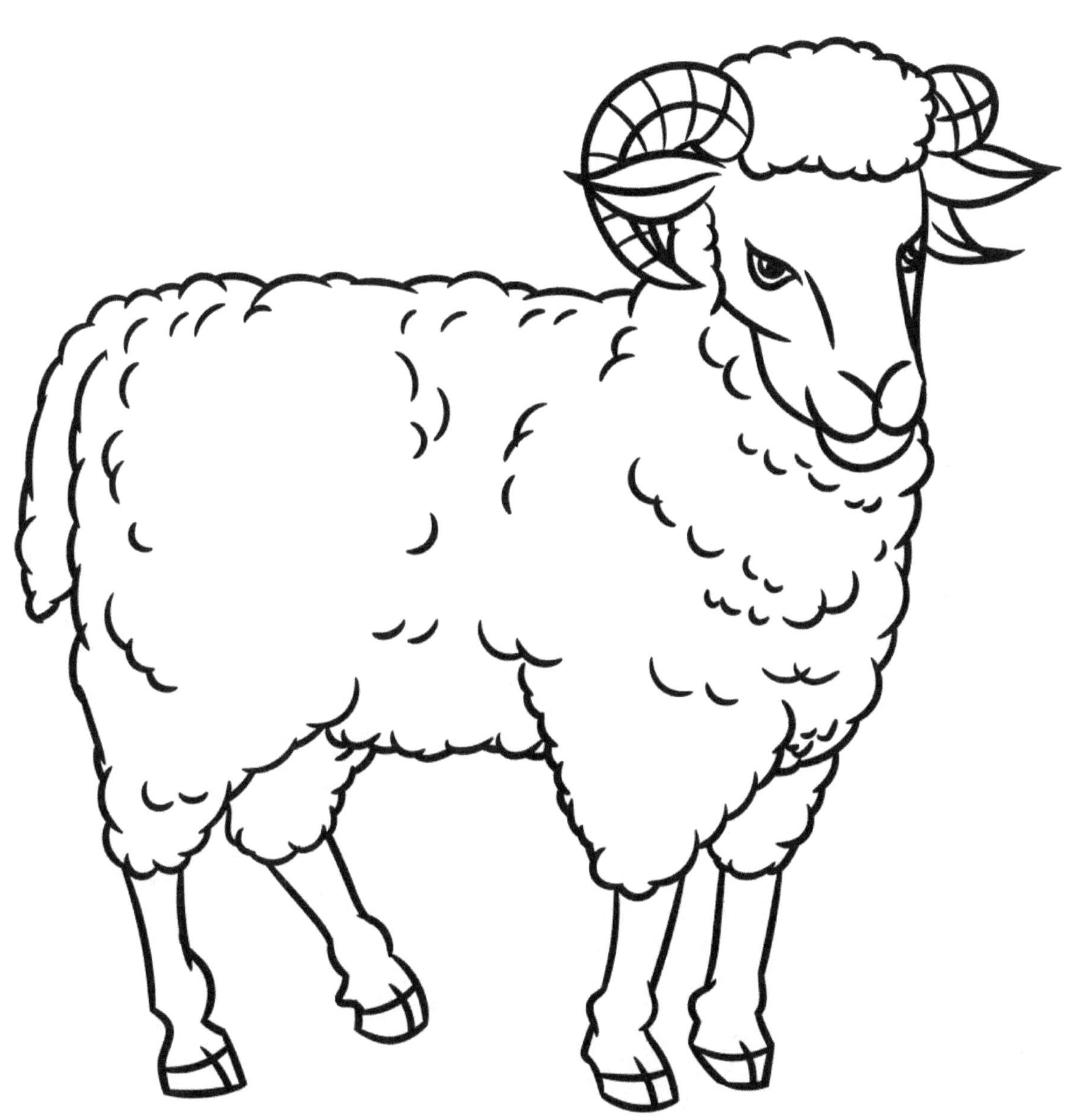

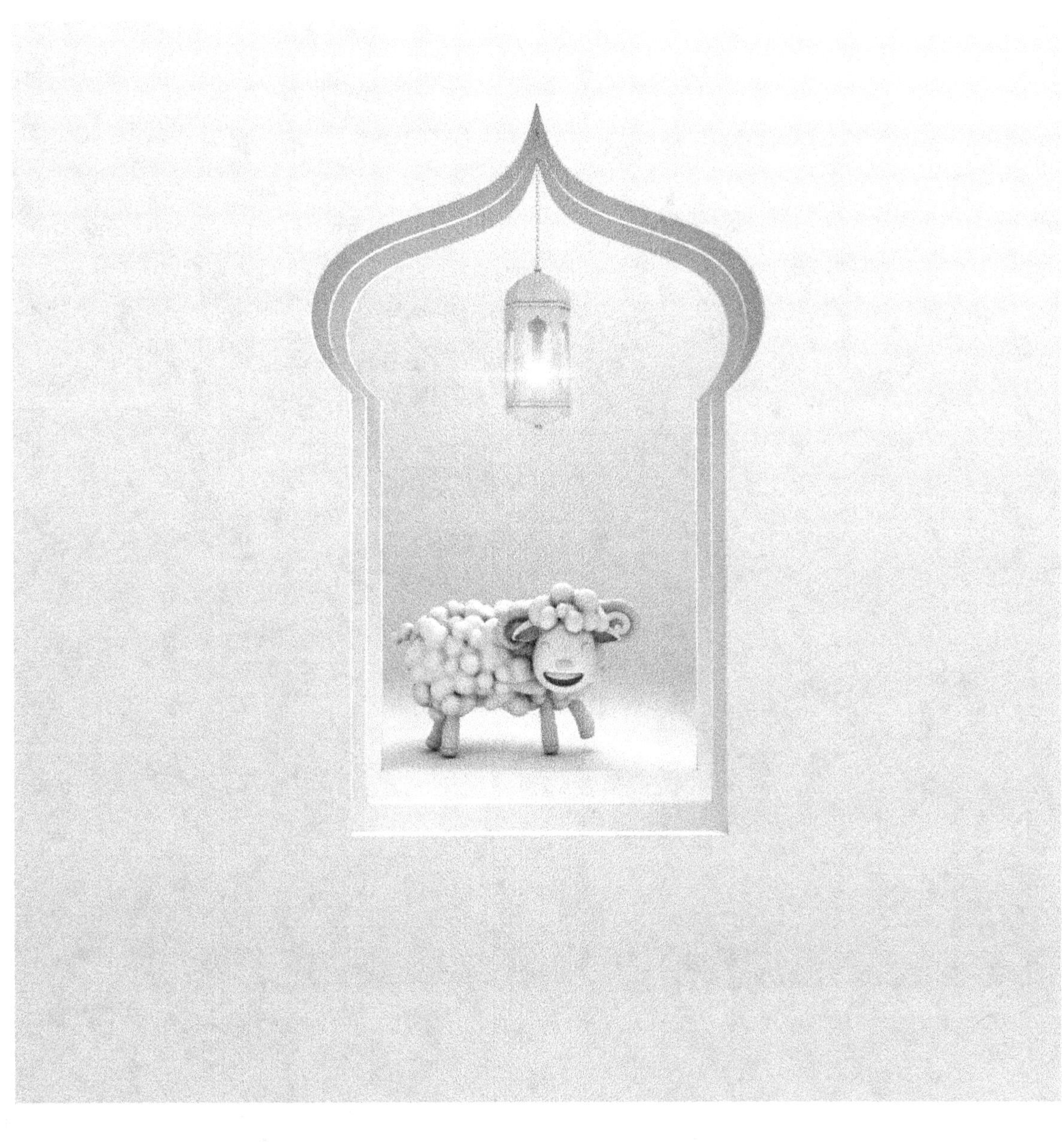

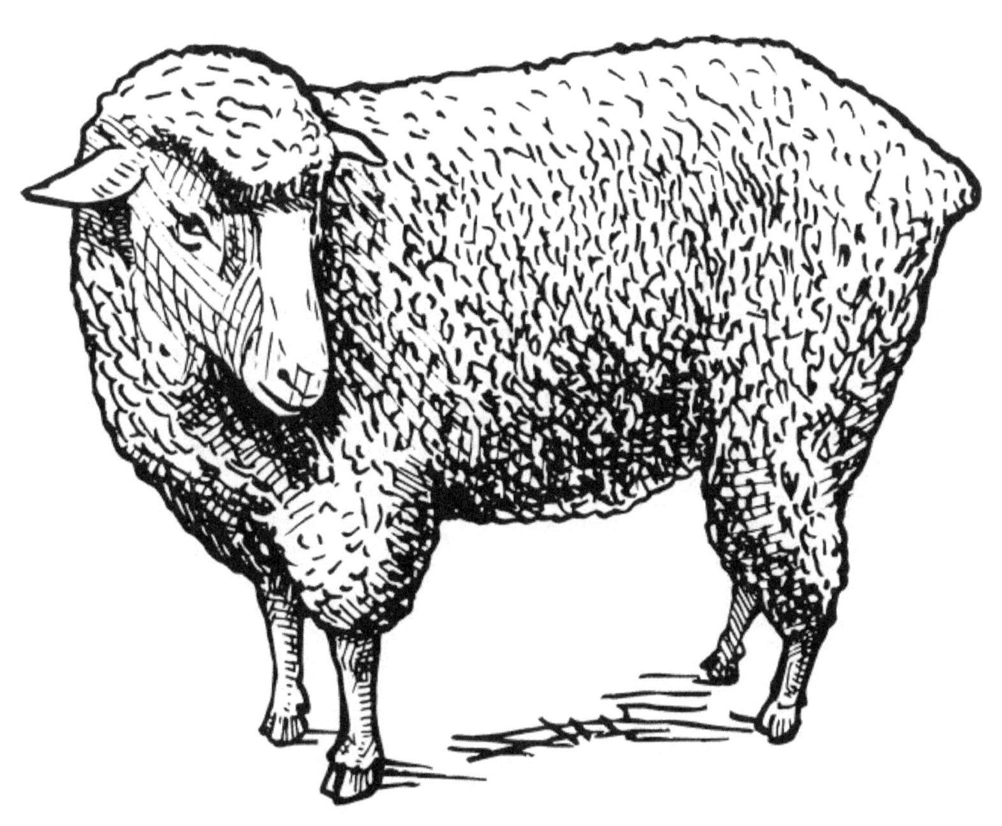

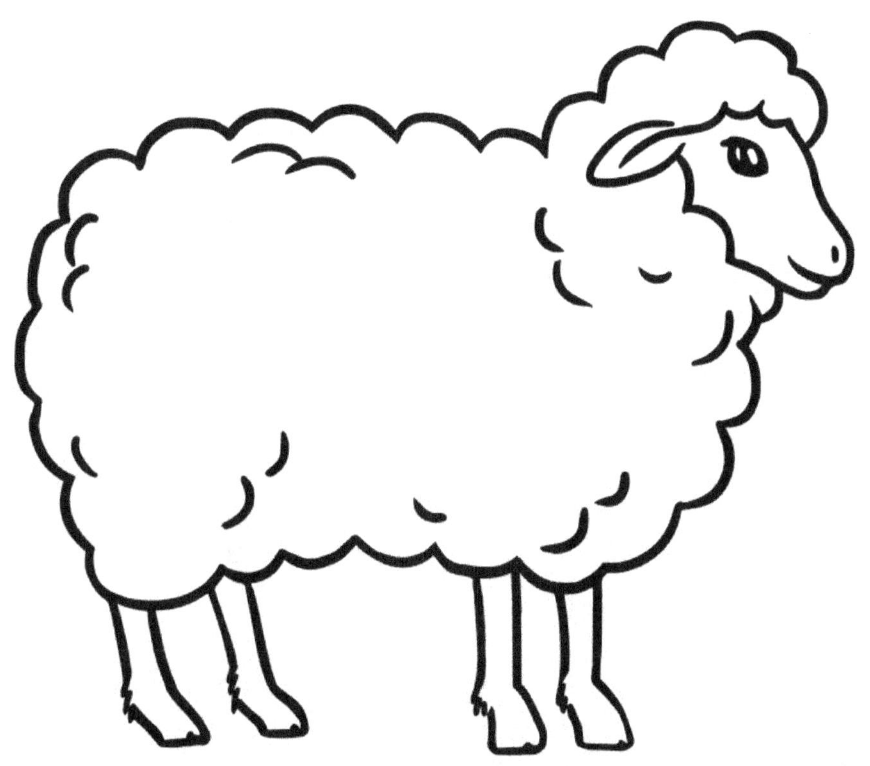

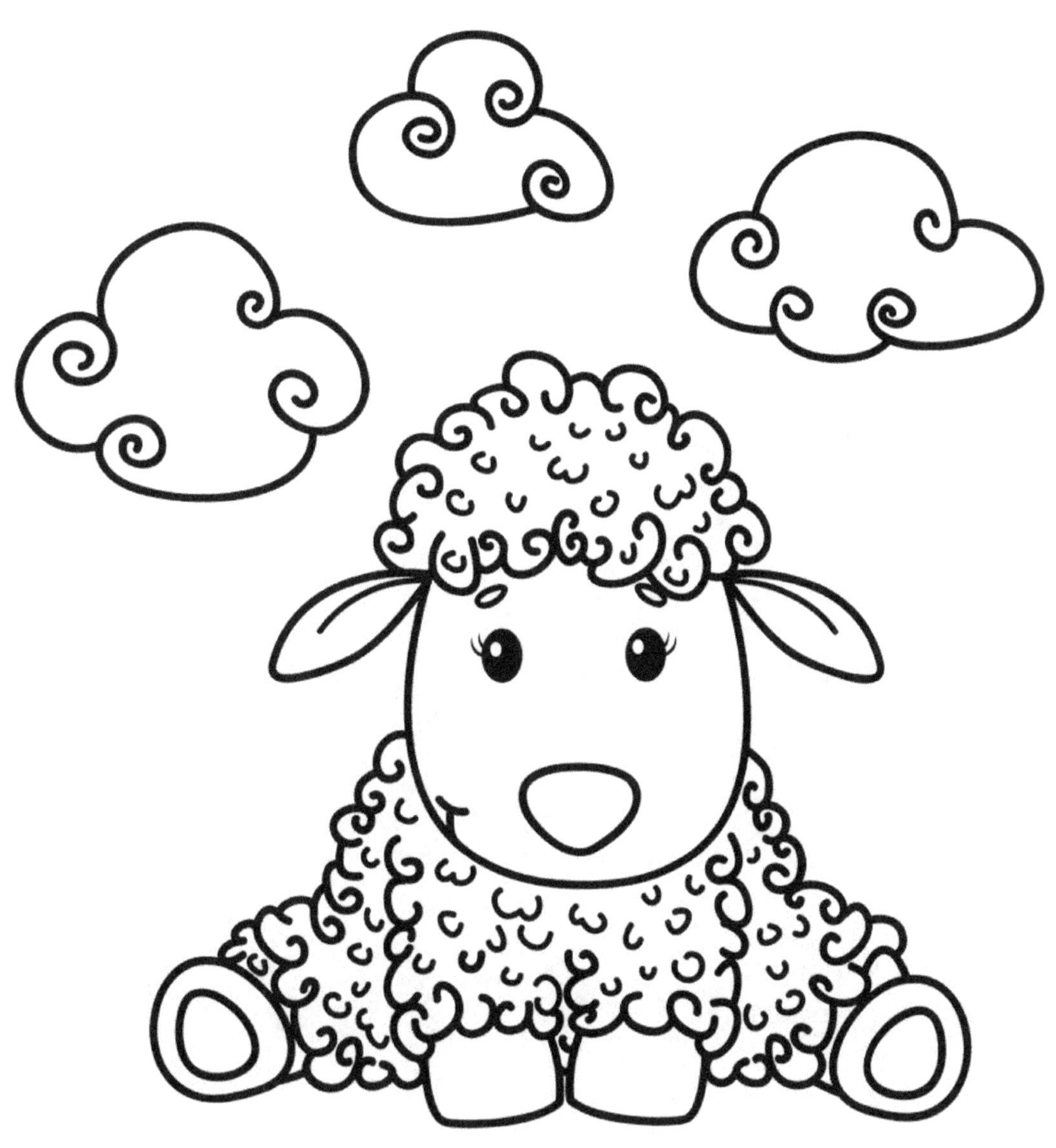

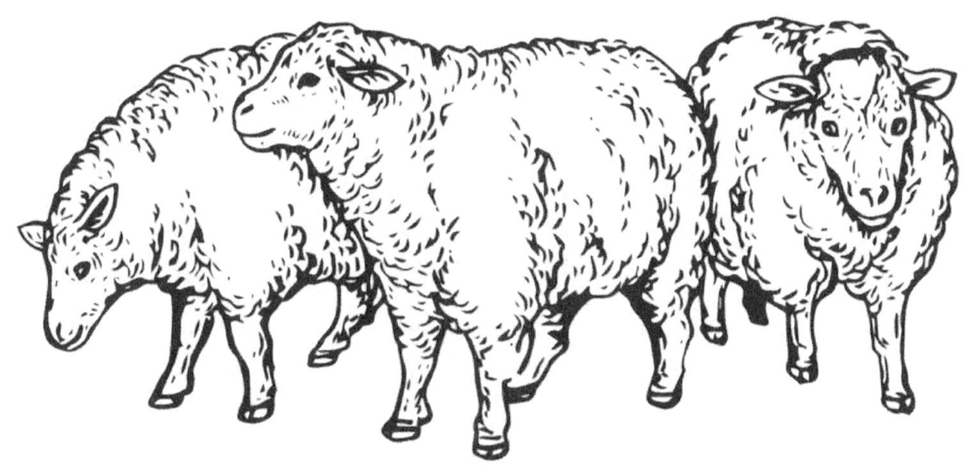

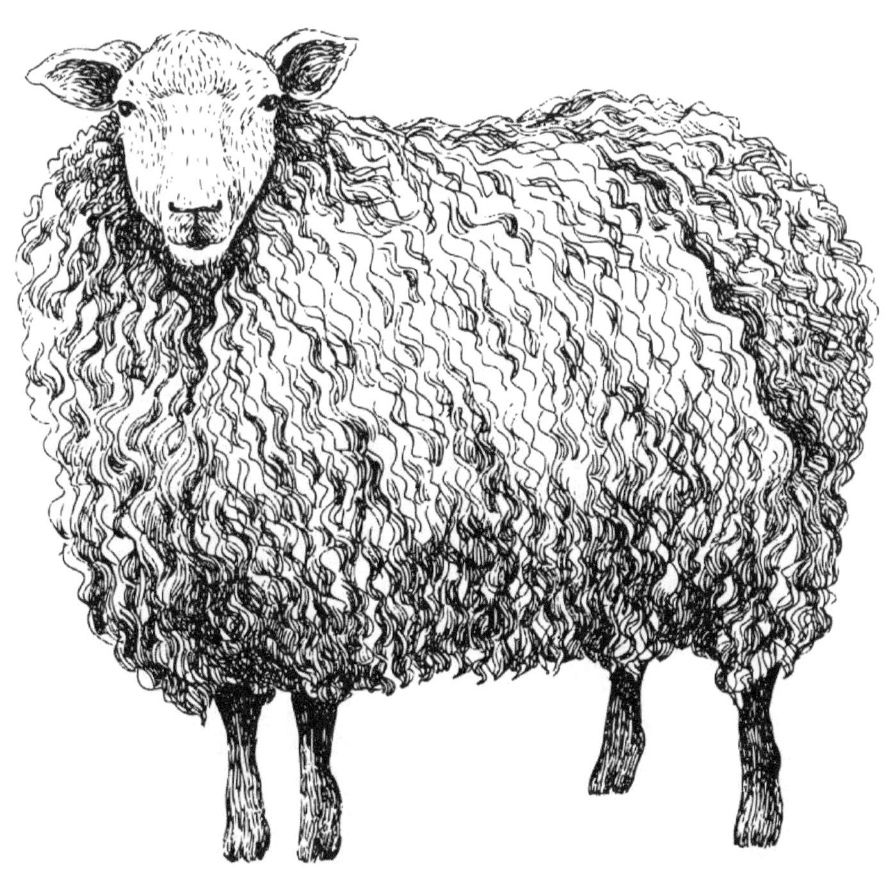

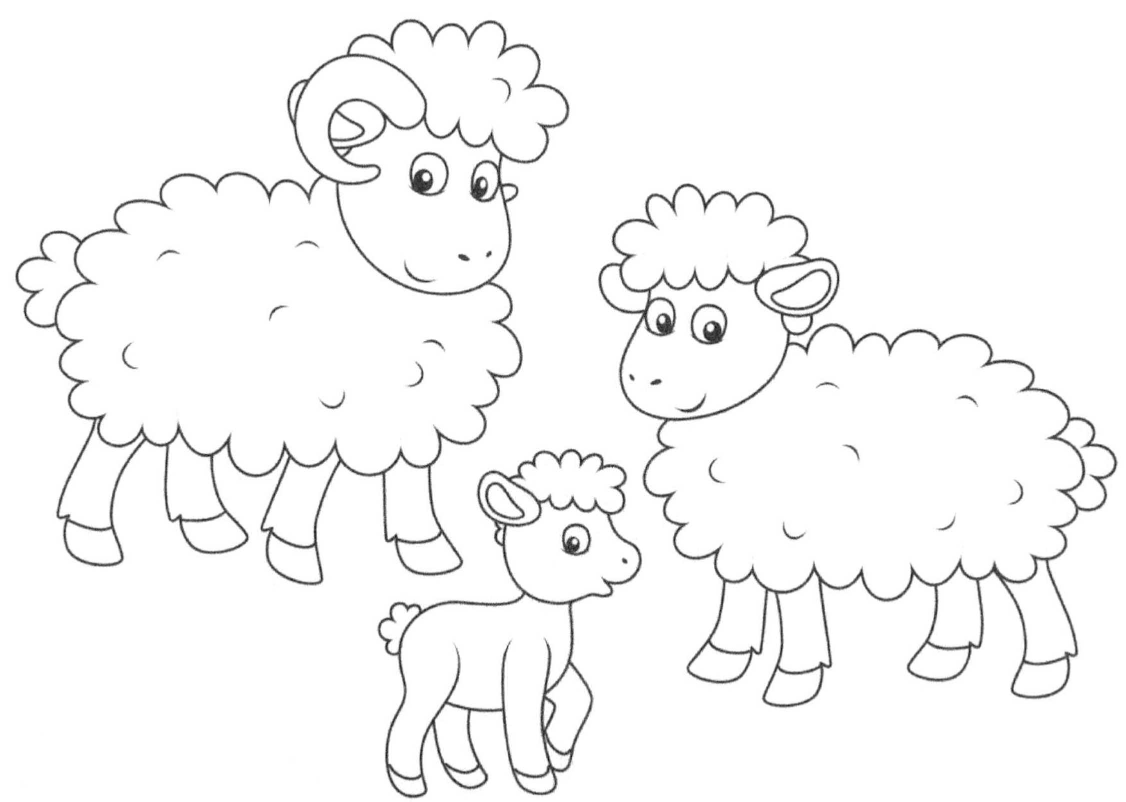

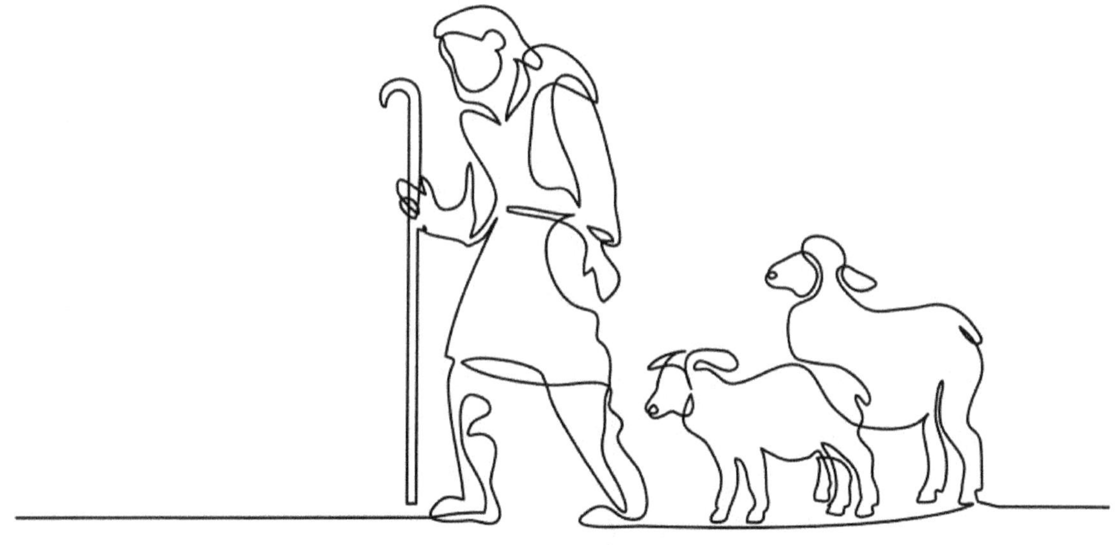

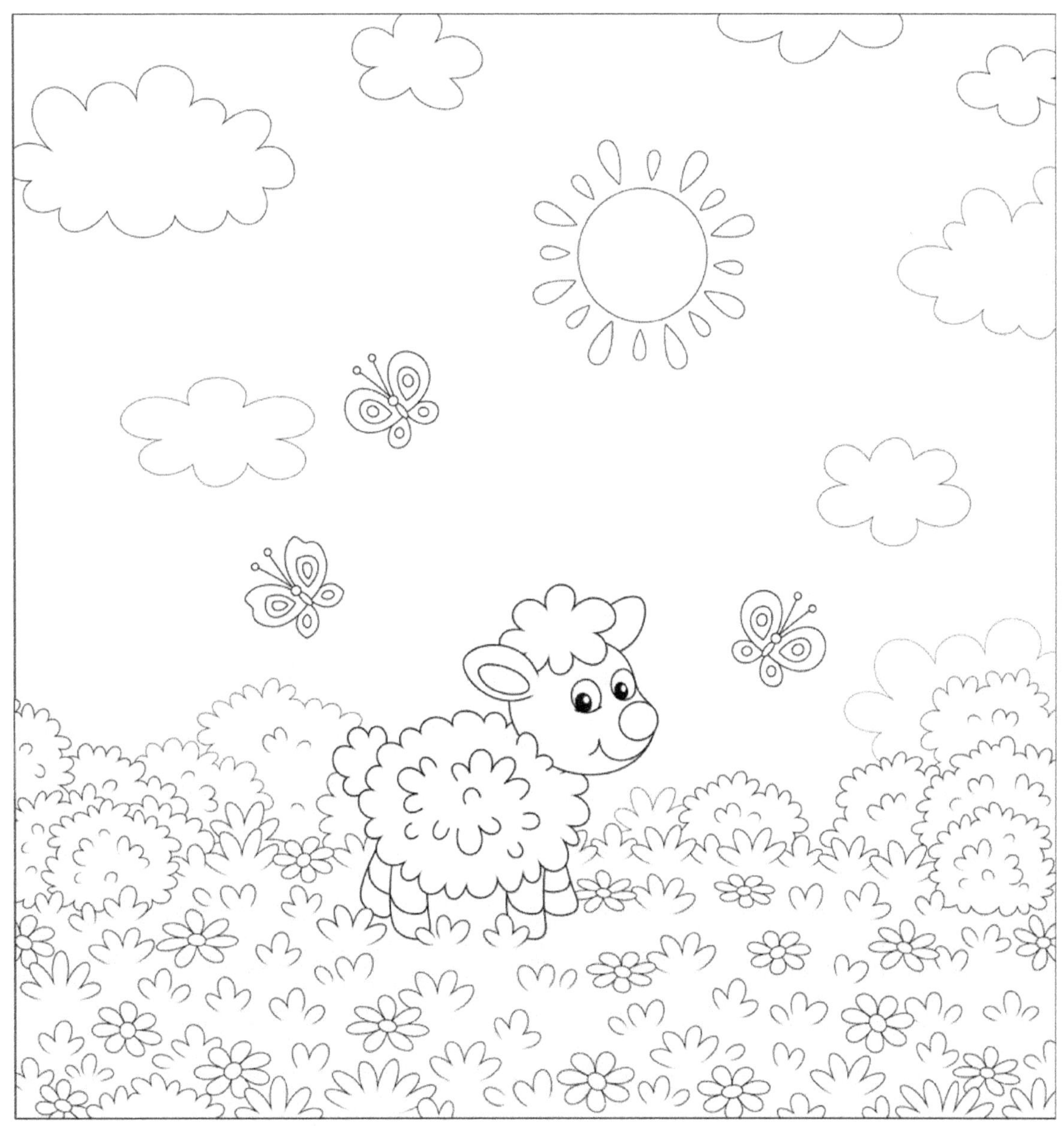

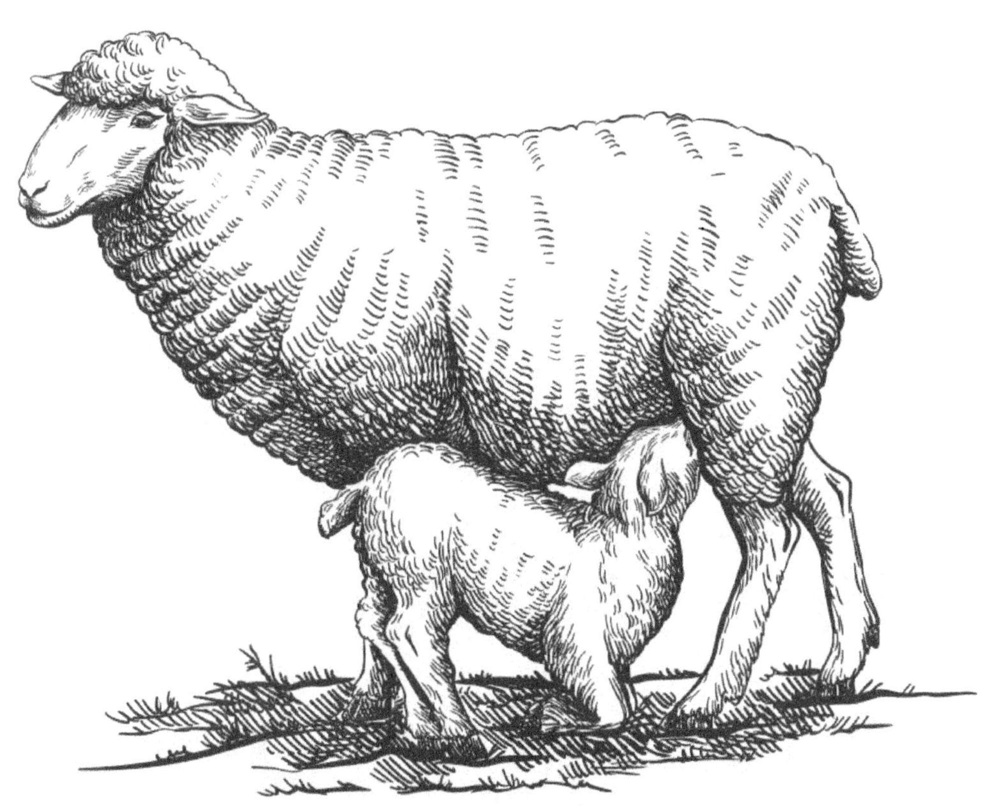

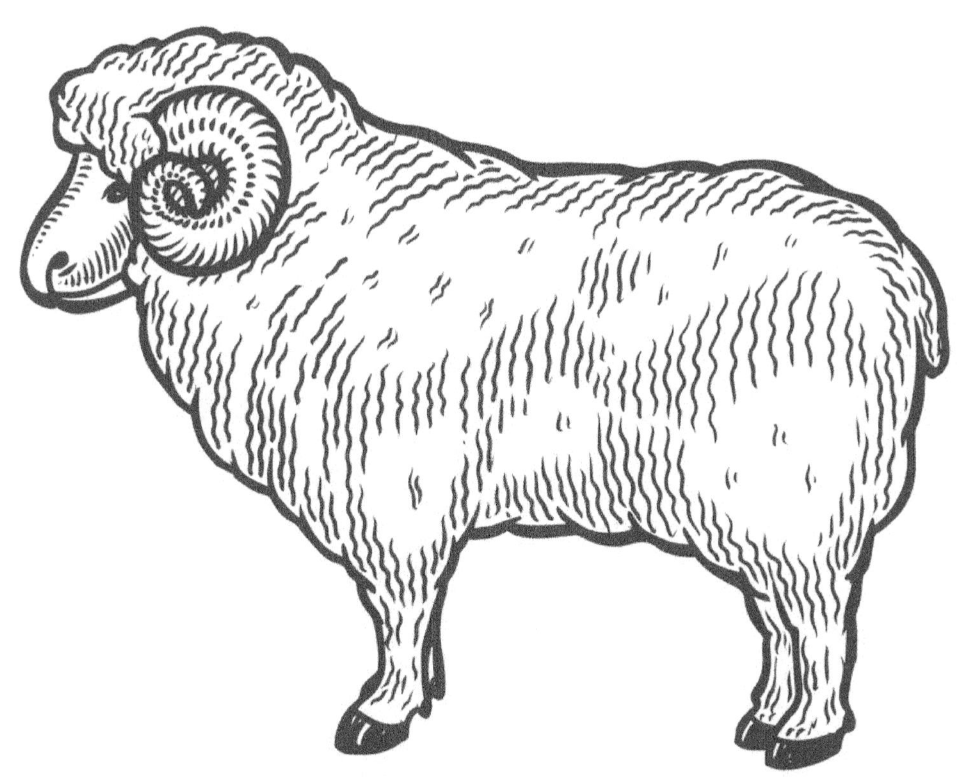

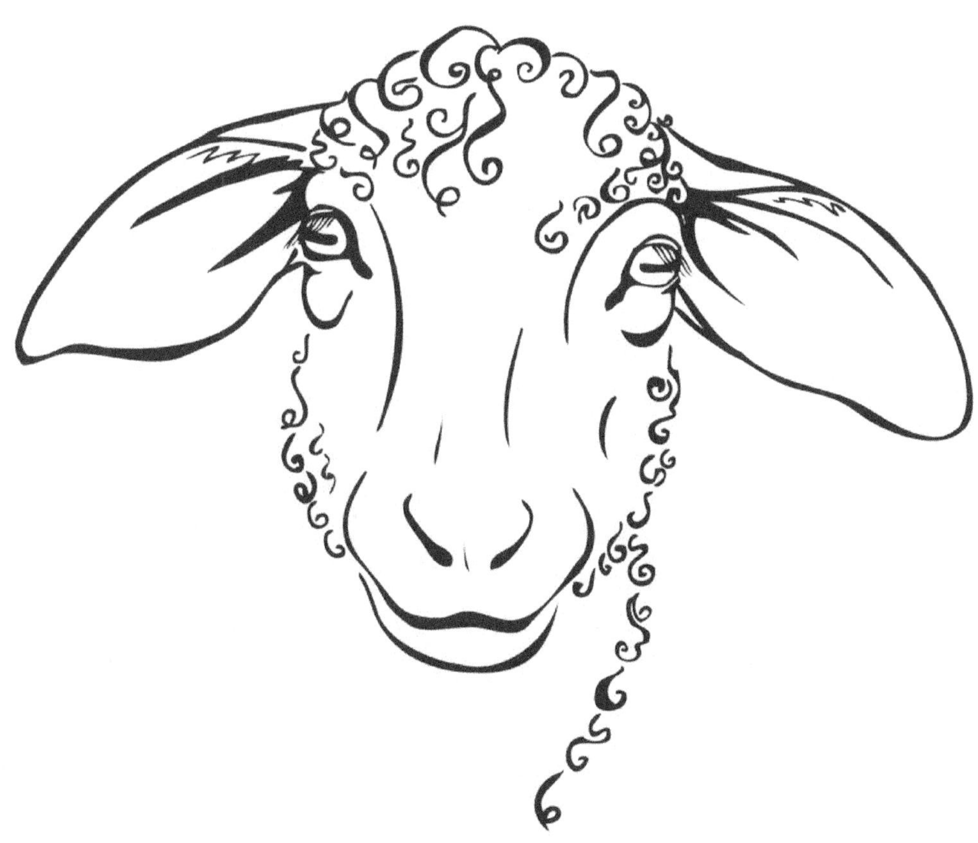

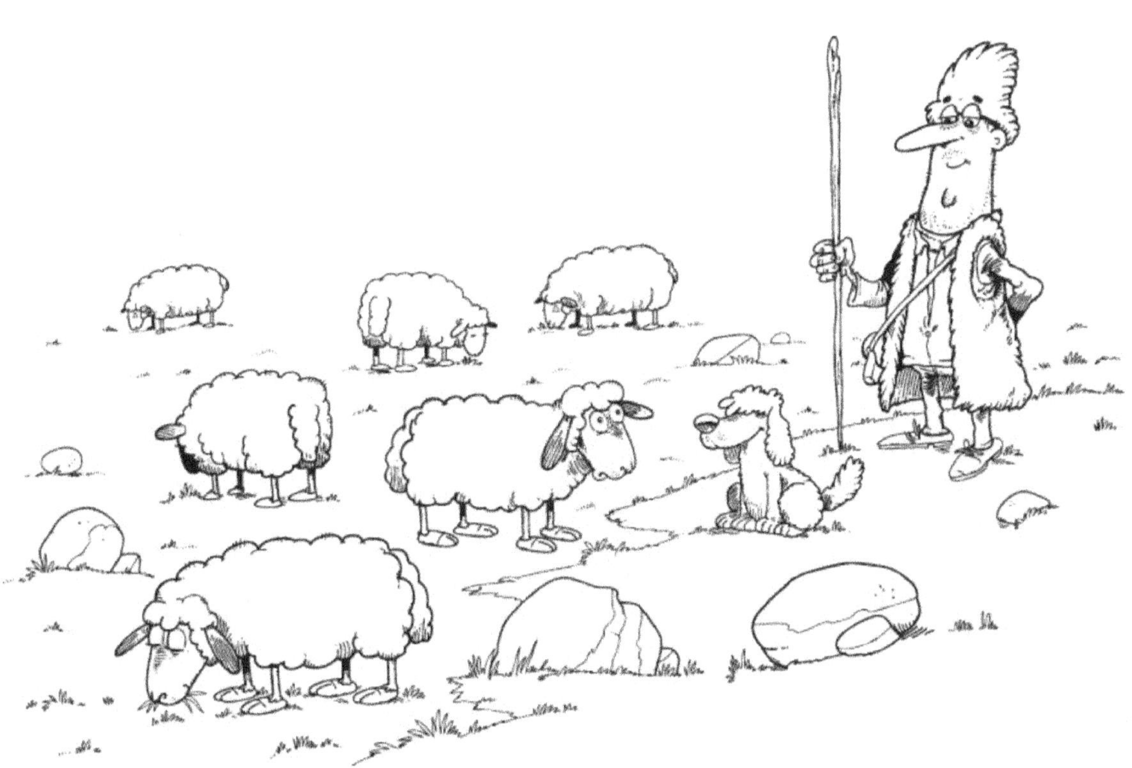

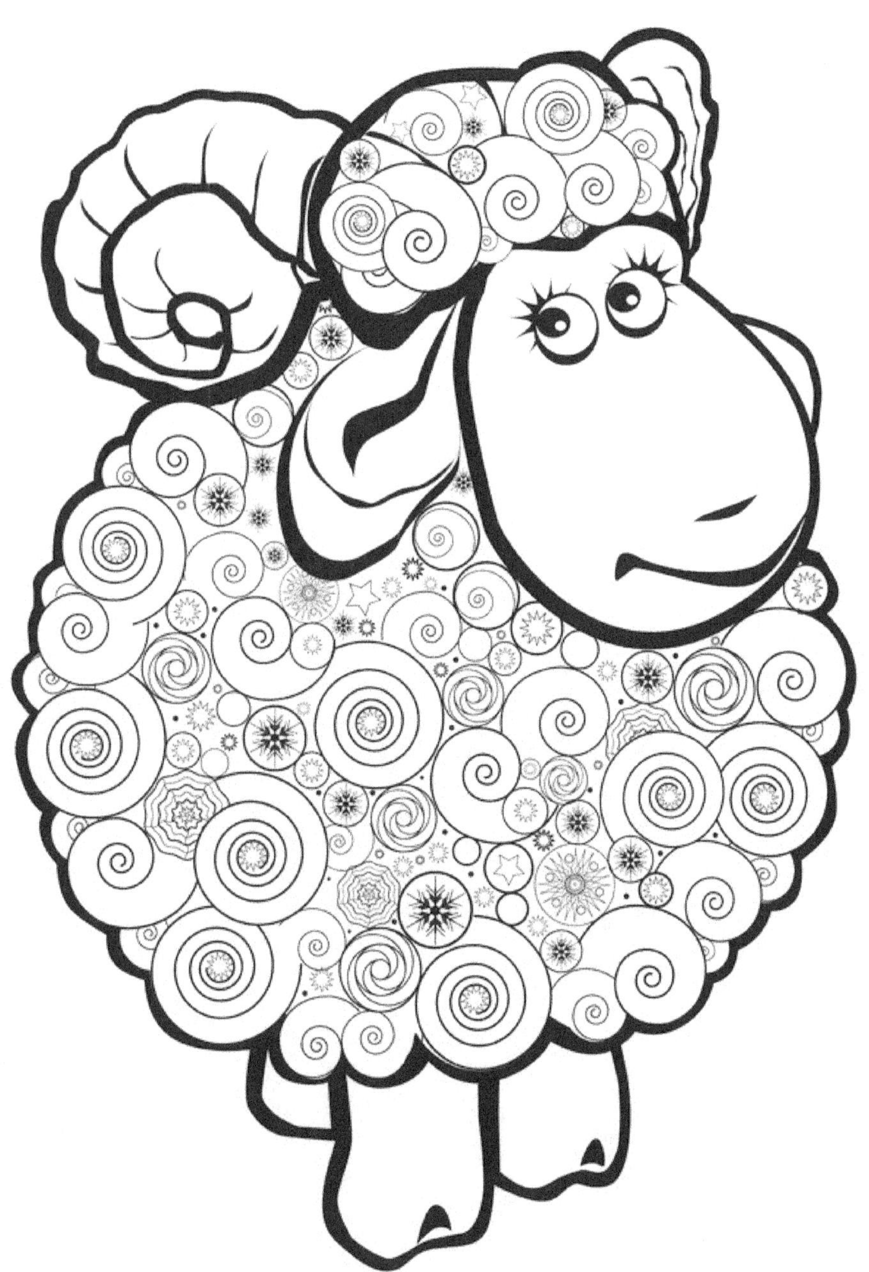

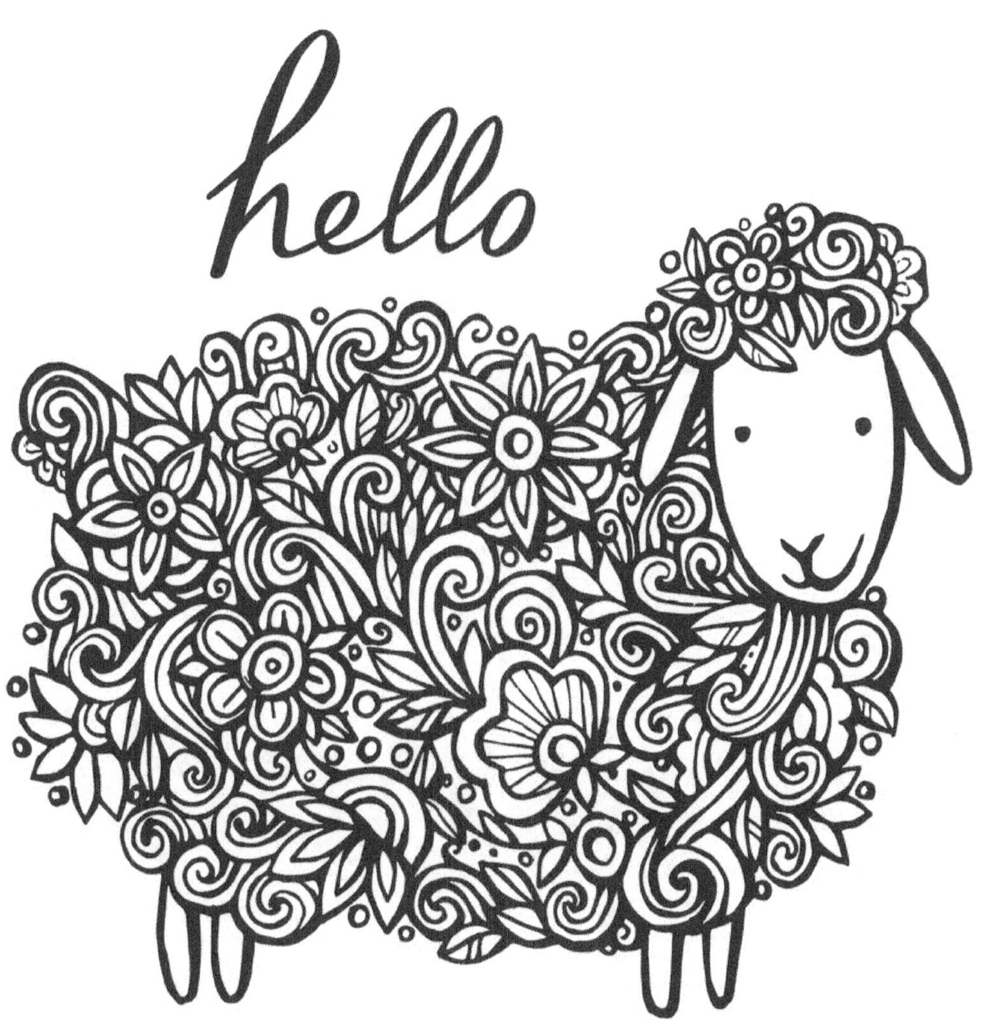

hello

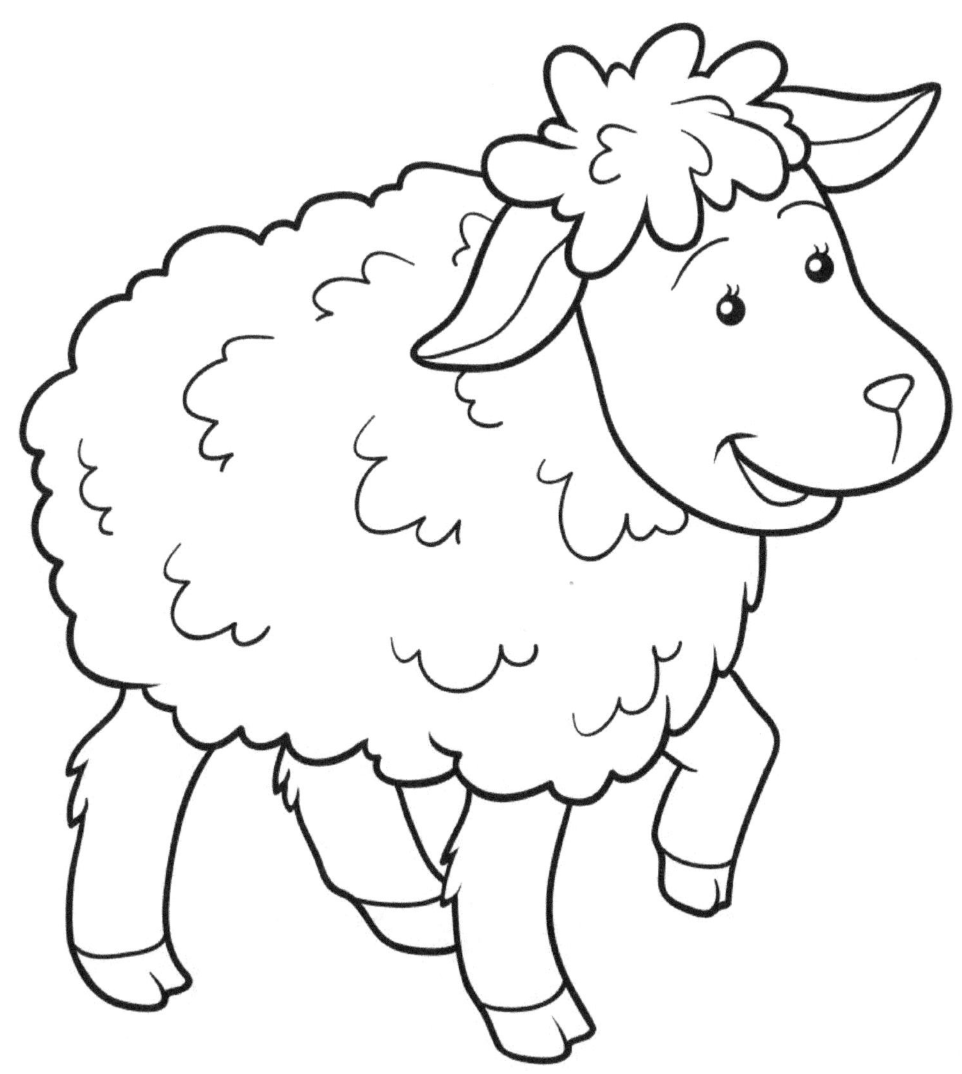

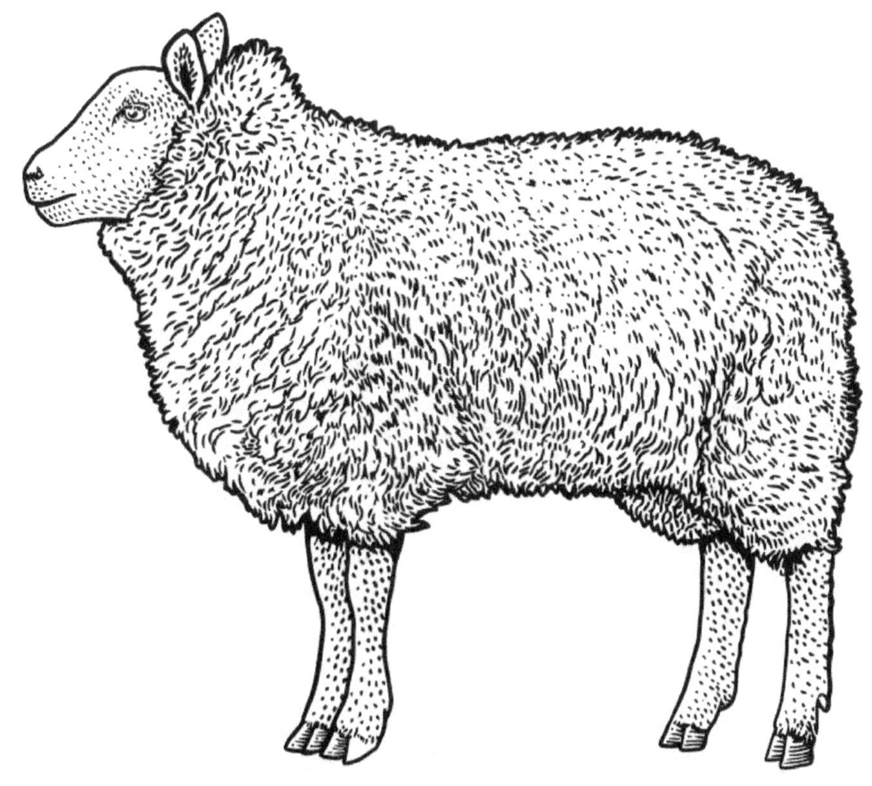

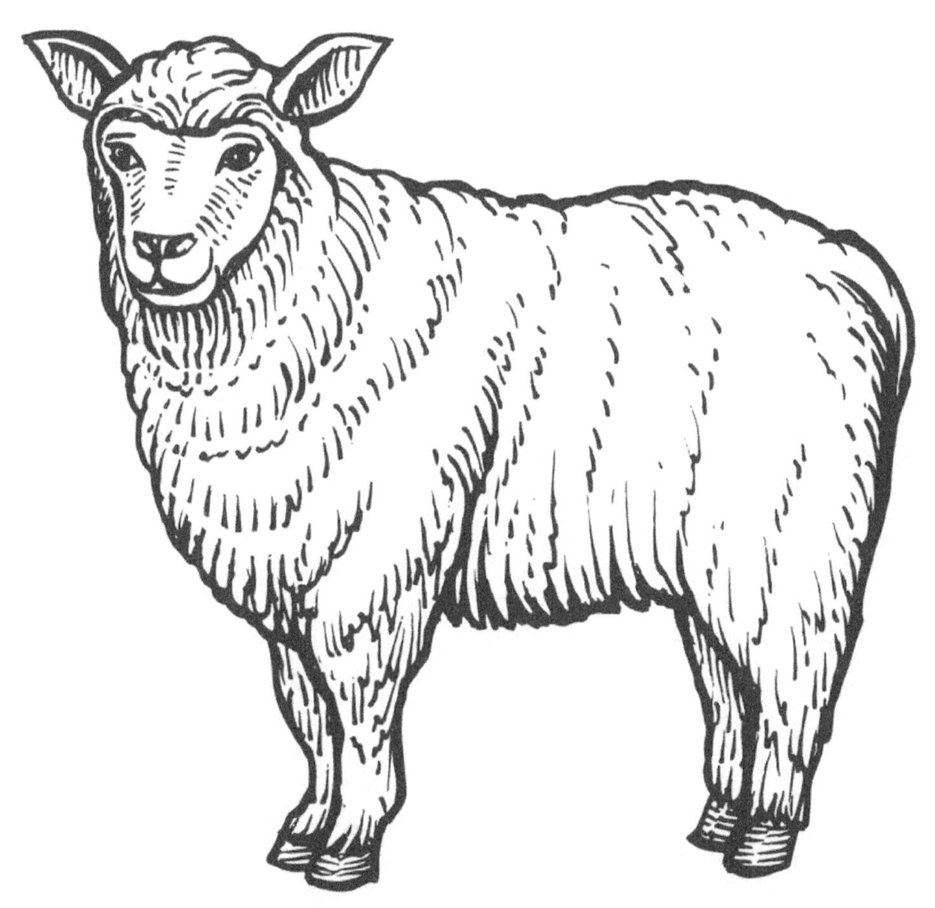

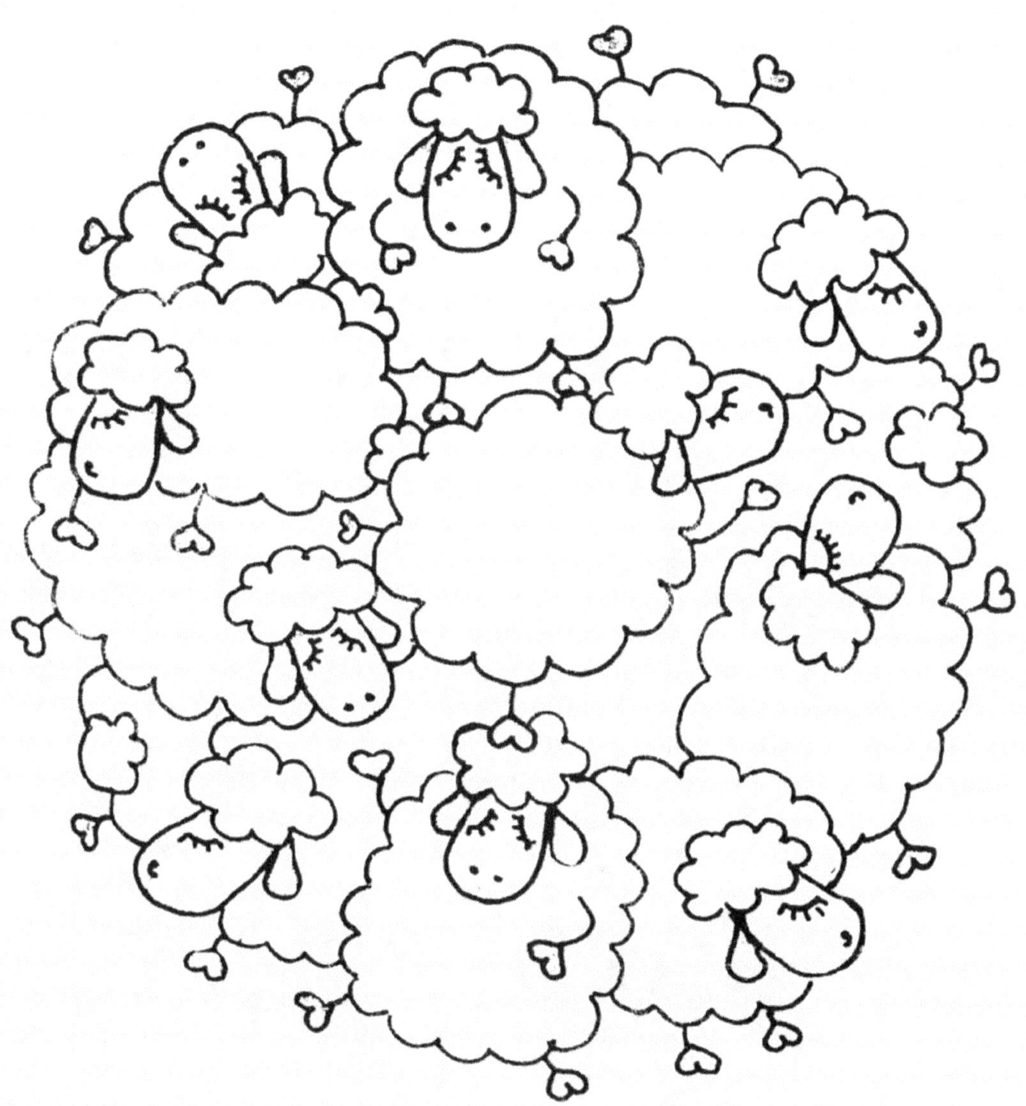

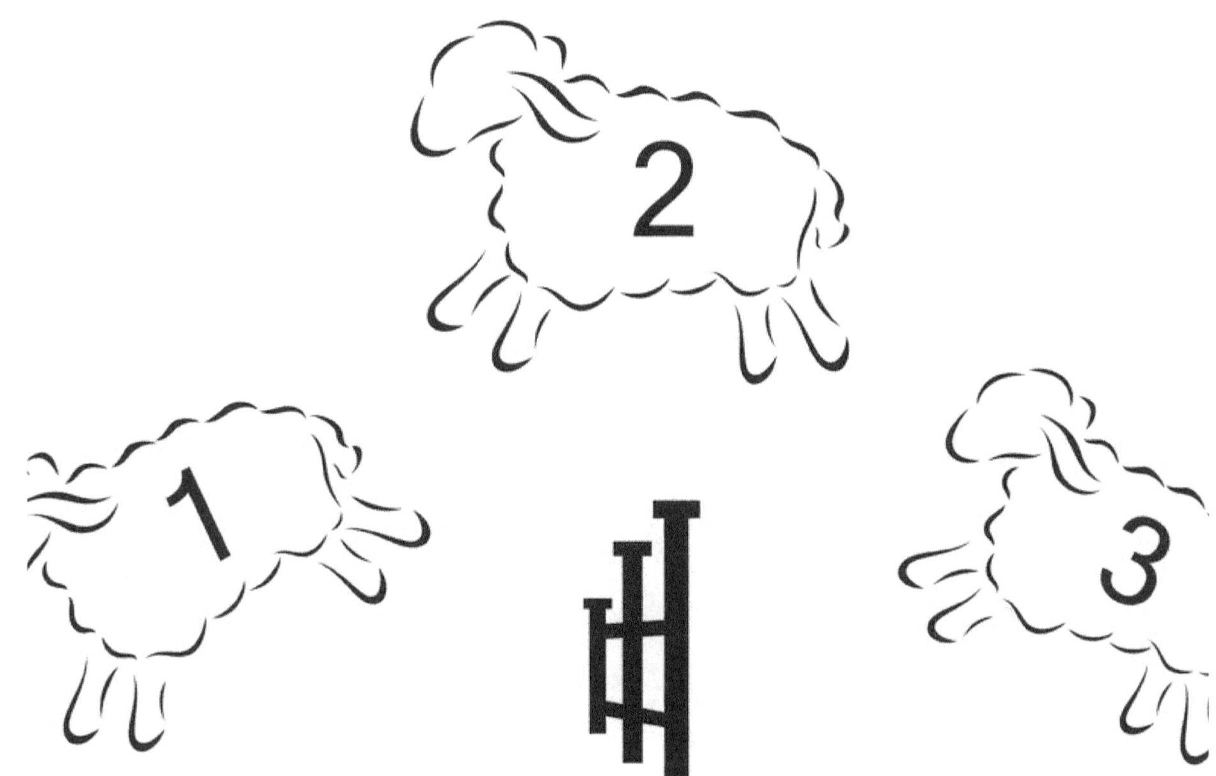

2
1
3

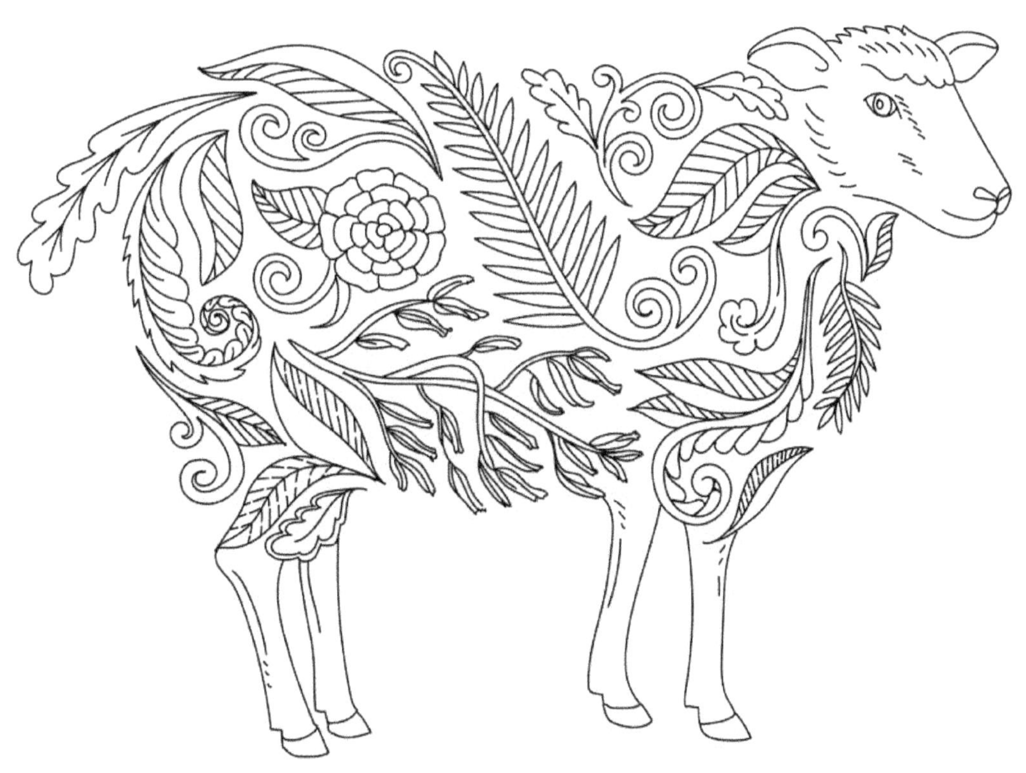

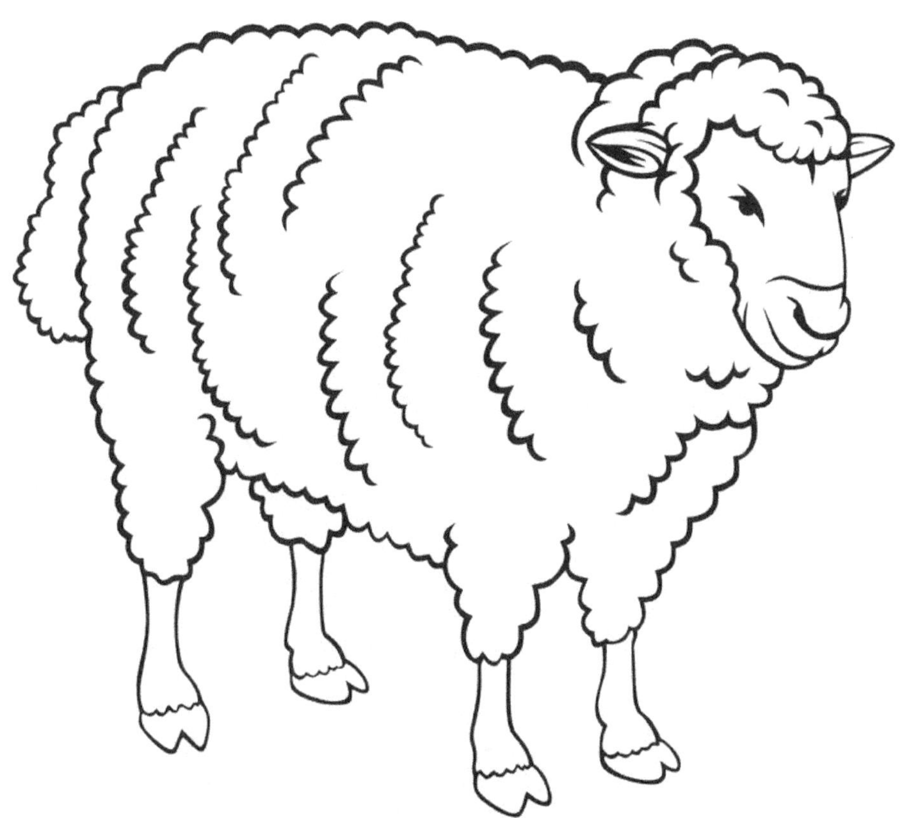

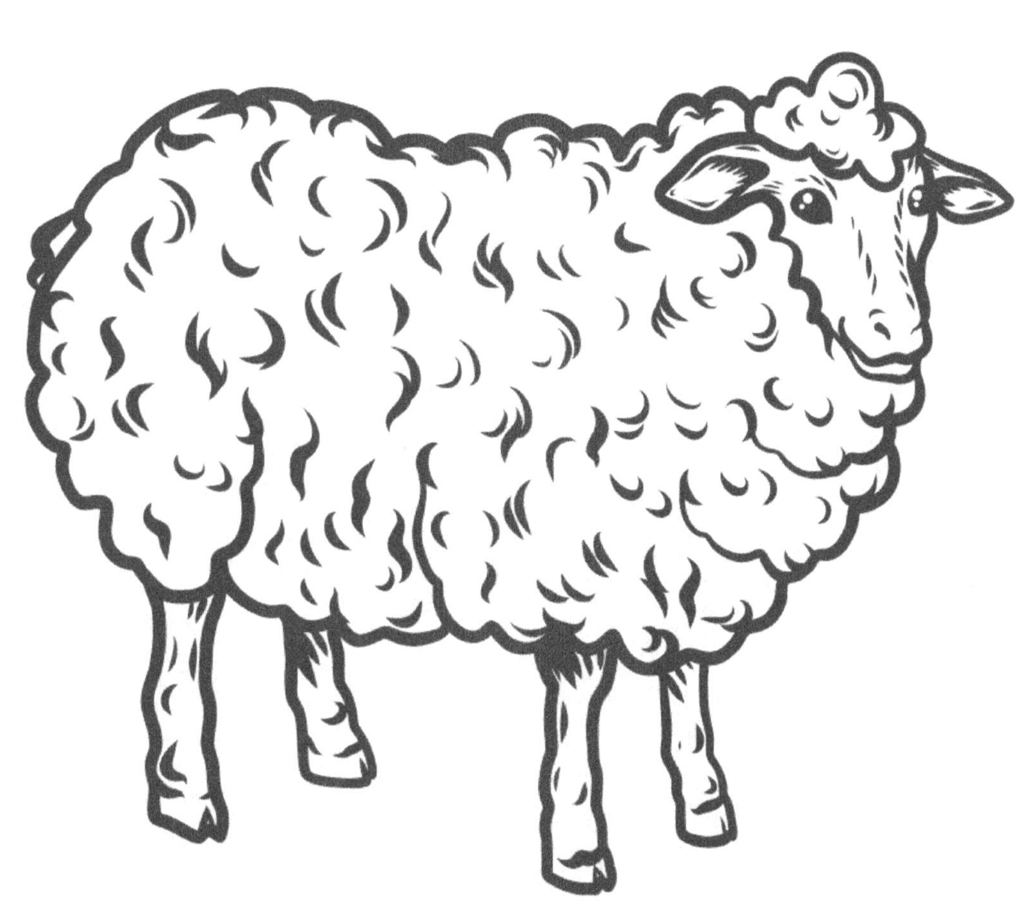

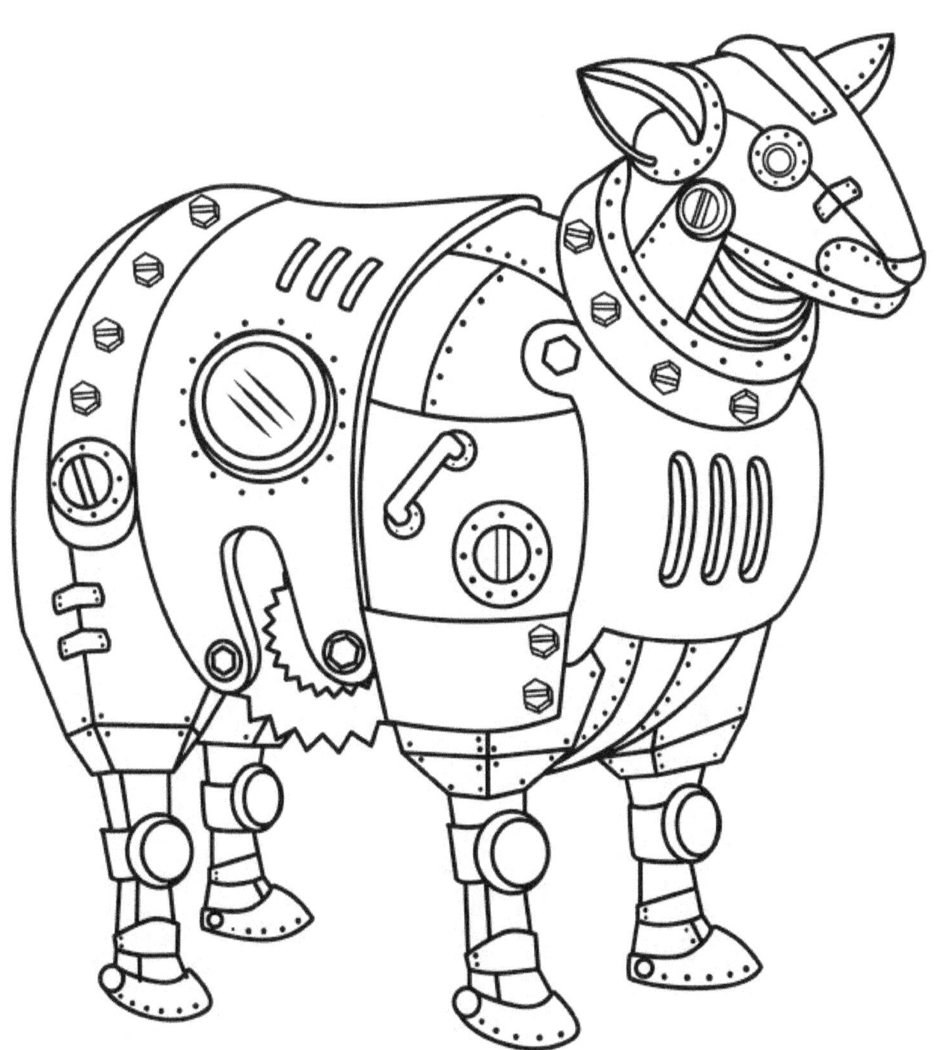

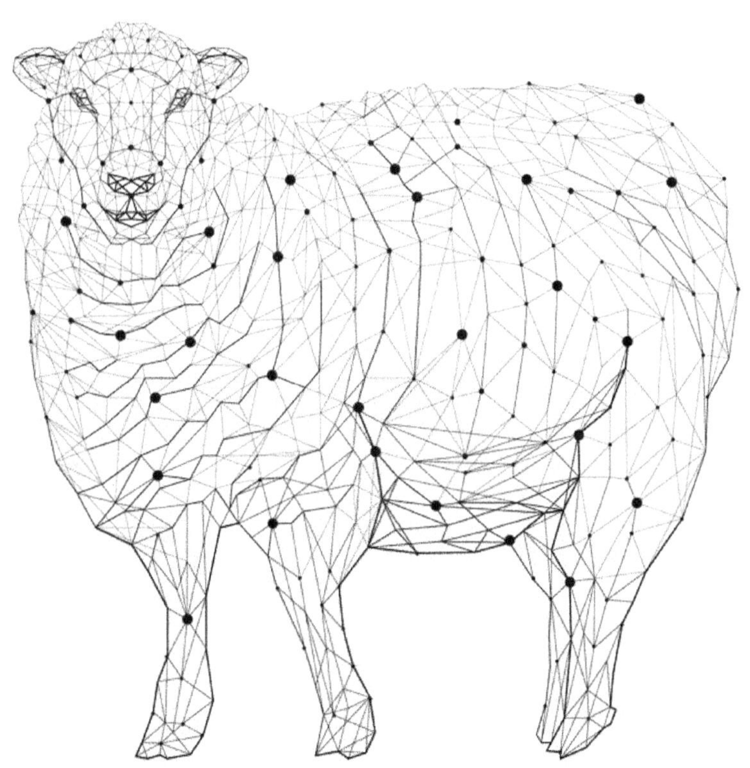

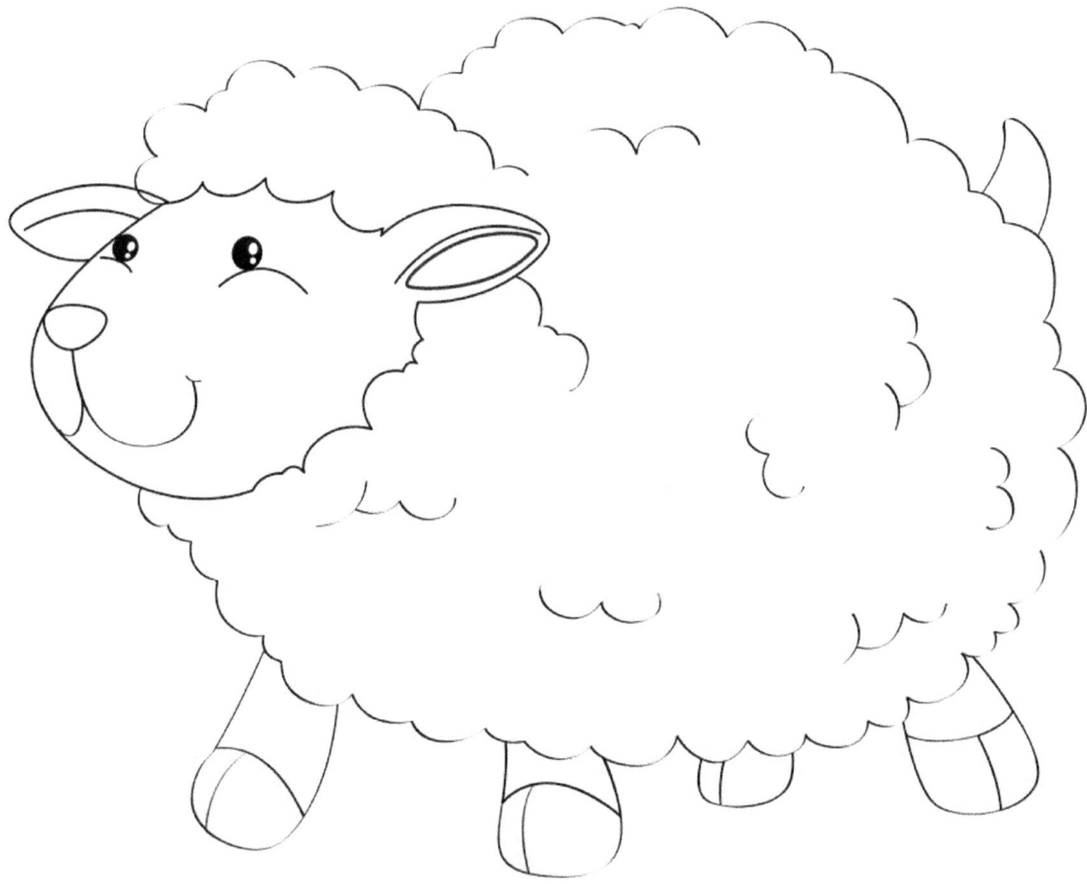

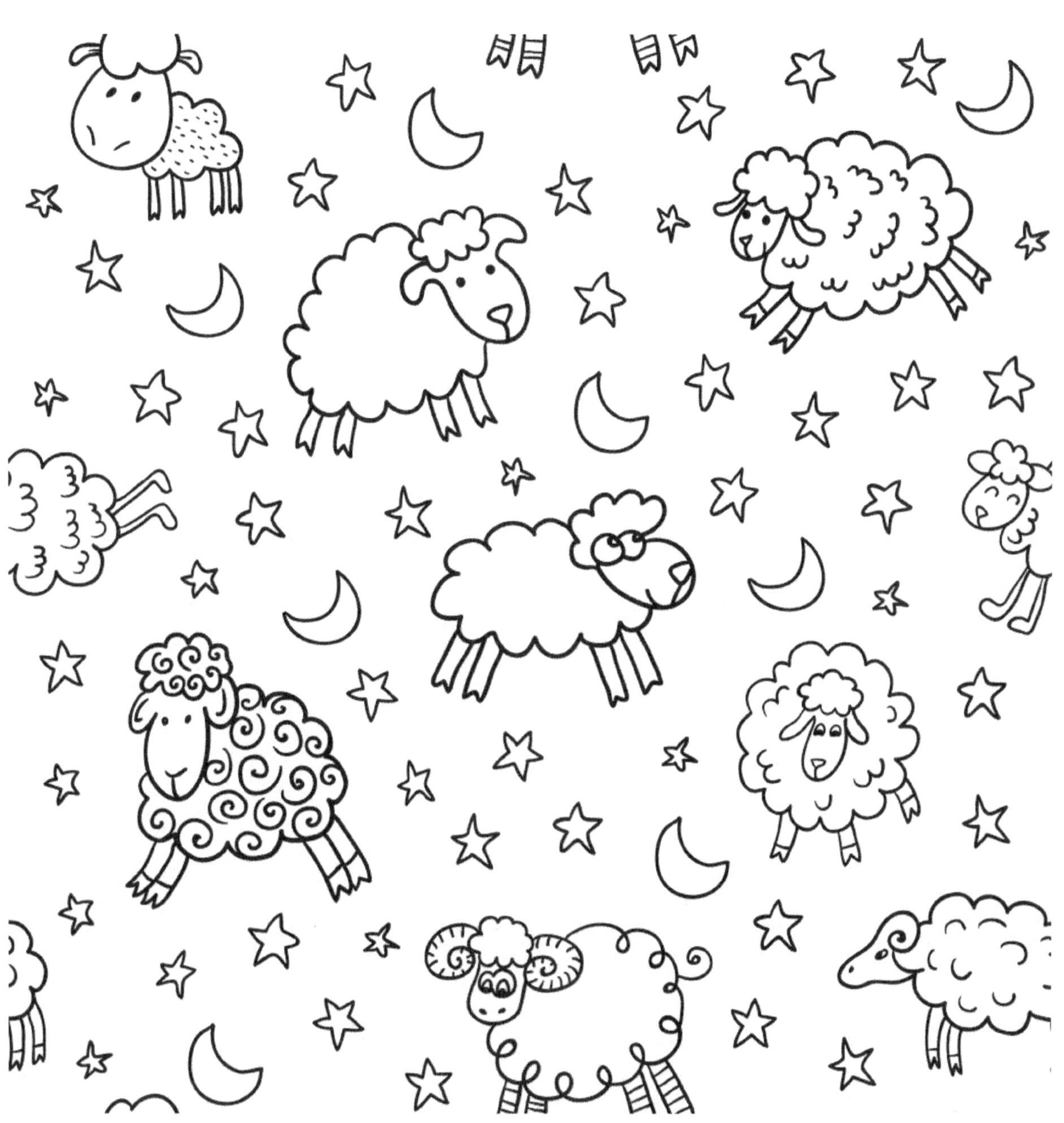